TAZ
& the Big Flappy Thing

TAZ

& The Big Flappy Thing

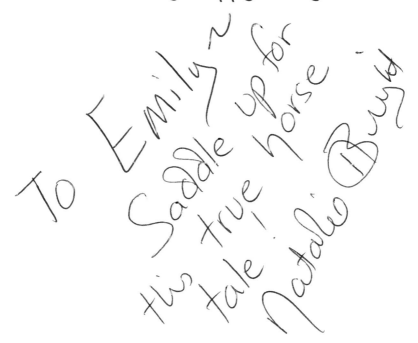

To Emily~
Saddle up for
his true horse
tale!
Natalie Bright

NATALIE BRIGHT

STEPHANIE NELSON

http://nataliebright.com

Published by NKB Books, LLC

EBook ISBN 978-0-9988101-2-6
Print ISBN 978-0-9988101-3-3

In Collaboration with Stephanie Nelson
Editor: Denise McAllister
Cover Design, Layout & Formatting by gessertbooks.com

DISCLAIMER

For any inquiries regarding this book, please email: natalie@nataliebright.com

DEDICATION

To the people who care for rescue animals, and my heartfelt thanks to Stephanie for introducing me to her amazing Hackney named Taz. **NKB**

To Terri Gammage, founder of Panhandle Safe Hayven Equine Rescue, and her husband Ronny, for their life-time dedication to saving horses and helping people. Terri told me, "I've got just the horse for you!" **ST**

CHAPTER 1

The black Hackney horse buried his nose in the tall grass growing in the road side ditch.

"After you eat, Taz, we are going to learn something new," said his owner, Stephanie.

Taz looked up from his munching. He loved learning. It kept his mind busy and he liked pleasing his human.

Stephanie led him to the barn. She tied his lead rope to the pipe fence and disappeared inside. When she returned, she carried a big flappy thing.

"This is a flag, Taz. You and I are going to ride in a parade. I will be carrying this." She held the flapping thing high. Taz took a good look.

His curious corral mate, Bly, inspected the striped fabric as it whipped in the breeze. She jerked her head away and spun around. She hurried to the other side of the pen.

"Looks like Bly does not like the flag," Stephanie laughed. "That leaves you and me, Taz. Can you do this for me?"

Taz stretched his nose a little closer. He lipped the fabric. Stephanie wrapped one corner of the striped material around his nose.

She walked around and around Taz as she carried the Stars and Stripes. The fabric billowed in the breeze and flapped next to his face.

Taz decided he did not like the big flappy thing, but he didn't run away like Bly had done.

Stephanie allowed Taz to sniff the flag one more time and then she rolled it securely around the pole. "We will work again tomorrow," she said.

The beautifully spotted Bly paid no attention to the lesson or the big flappy thing.

Stephanie gave Taz a pat on the neck and filled his feed bucket. Stephanie's daughter, Lachelle, held the bucket for him. Taz soon forgot about the new thing that had invaded his space. He concentrated on his grain.

CHAPTER 2

On Saturday, the next morning, Taz heard the bump of the back door. He watched Lachelle walk toward the barn. She soon appeared at the corral carrying the flag on a long pole.

He greeted her at the fence holding his feed bucket between his teeth.

"Good morning, Bly," Lachelle said. "Good morning, Taz."

She rewarded each with a scratch between the ears and a horse cookie.

"Taz, we need to talk," Lachelle said. "Mom wants you to walk in a parade."

The registered Hackney sniffed his favorite human's hair with a loud snort.

"There is no reason to be afraid," she said.

He nudged her shoulder with his nose.

"No, sir. You may not have another cookie," said Lachelle. "I am trying to tell you what I learned in school. That flag has 50 stars – one for each state in the country."

Taz backed up a step. He suddenly remembered that he did not like that flappy thing.

Lachelle put her hand on his hard-muscled neck. "I know you don't like it now, but you will learn. It's got seven red stripes and six white stripes." She unrolled the flag from around the pole. "Look. It's very pretty."

The black horse shook his head, his mane swirled with the motion.

"You have to carry mom and the flag downtown," Lachelle told him. "I know you can do it."

The back door of their house echoed again with a loud bang.

"Here she comes," said Lachelle as Taz gave her neck a snuggle. "Please try."

Taz watched his other favorite human walk to the barn. She took that ridiculous flappy thing from Lachelle.

"Are you ready to start training for the parade, Taz?" asked Stephanie.

Taz looked at Lachelle, and then he looked at Stephanie. He did not see any way out of this. They had him outnumbered.

CHAPTER 3

The next training session with the flag began
where the last one had ended. Stephanie
showed Taz the flag. He lipped it and sniffed it.
She walked around and around him as she held
the flag high.

This time she slowly and gently laid the Stars and Stripes across his back. Taz stiffened and froze. Two very important questions came to his mind: *Will it eat me? Can it hurt me?*

Both Lachelle and Stephanie encouraged him.

Lachelle reminded him how important his job would be on parade day.

"You can do this, Taz," Stephanie told him in a calm, reassuring voice.

Taz could tell that Stephanie was not afraid of the flag. Lachelle did not fear the big flappy thing either.

Why was he so scared?

Stephanie rode Taz while she held the flag. They rode around and around the pasture.

Taz worked hard over the next four weeks. He tried to understand the job that Stephanie needed him to do. He felt the big flappy thing touch him again and again.

Day after day it flapped in the wind, whipping and whirling over his head.

Taz did not like being scared.

He calmed and understood that the flag was not anything to be frightened of.

"I think you are ready for parade day, Taz," Stephanie told him one evening. "There will be people and floats, and strange things you have never seen before. Just remember, I will not let anything hurt you."

Taz still was not sure about this thing called a parade, but if Stephanie would be there, he felt alright with the idea.

CHAPTER 4

The day finally arrived.

Parade day!

It was time to load up.

"It is time to go, Taz," said Lachelle. "I know you can do this."

As the trailer pulled onto the paved black top, the horse watched Lachelle wave to him from their driveway.

He and Stephanie traveled to the city.

"Here we are, Taz," said Stephanie as she backed him out of the trailer. "Downtown. We are riding in the Veteran's Day Parade today."

Other members of the Randall County Sheriff's Posse Mounted Search and Rescue Team were unloading nearby.

"Oh, no," Stephanie said. "I can't believe I forgot your bit and bridle. Maybe I can borrow one. I'll be right back." She tied Taz to the trailer.

Stephanie disappeared in the cluster of horses, riders, pickup trucks, and livestock trailers.

"Try this," Stephanie said to Taz when she returned. "I know that it is one more strange thing on top of everything else, but we will have to make it work."

With a borrowed bridle on his head, the bit felt odd in Taz's mouth. He kept pushing on it with his tongue. The new surroundings and a different bit in his mouth added to his nervousness.

His red saddle blanket, red polo wraps, and red reins looked good against his shiny coat. Taz felt fancy in his posse gear. He was a little nervous, but Stephanie was right by his side. He was ready.

CHAPTER 5

In a parking lot in downtown Amarillo, Stephanie steered Taz around pickup trucks, trailers and people on horses. They followed the group of Sheriff's Posse members.

Taz gazed at a high school marching band. Strange squeaks and blasts of musical notes startled him as he passed.

They walked between two military floats with more flappy things. They rode next to a group of tap dancers all dressed alike in tie-dyed shirts.

They cut across another parking lot next to a high-rise office building. With eyes alert and ears perked, Taz shied away from the Khiva mules. He had never seen a mule before.

The next strange and horrible thing was a furry, humped-back creature. It looked huge. Taz rolled his eyes and side-stepped away from the strange animal.

"That is a stuffed camel on top of a float. He is not real," said Stephanie in a calm and reassuring voice. "You're doing okay, Taz." She kept a firm grip on the reins.

The Sheriff's Posse fell in line behind a wooden wagon pulled by two sturdy mules. Someone handed Stephanie a flag.

"This is a military flag, Taz," she said. "We are representing the United States Air Force today. My uncle was in the Air Force. Now we just have to be patient until it is our turn to go."

Taz felt a little jumpy, but confident that he could do his job. He watched the crowd with a hyper-awareness of everything around him. He sensed that Stephanie was calm. It was a good day to be riding on Polk Street in a parade.

"Here we go," said Stephanie. She squeezed with her legs. "We only have two miles to ride. You can do this."

People stood on both sides of the street. They all waved American flags. Big smiles and happy faces greeted Taz as he passed them.

The parade moved slowly. Several times they had to stop and wait. Taz did not want to stand in the middle of the street while everyone stared at him. He wanted to keep going.

They patiently waited for the wagon in front of them to start moving.

CHAPTER 6

Strange sites, musical notes, and crowds of people surrounded Taz on every side along the parade route in downtown Amarillo.

"Hang in there, Taz," Stephanie said. "We only have another mile to go."

Suddenly, there it was.

The scariest thing he had ever seen.

Alongside the curb, moving in the street, a man pushed a cart full of big floaty things.

BALLOONS!

Taz froze. His ears pricked. He stood alert, watching and wondering if those dreadful things would eat him. They were coming straight towards him.

Stephanie squeezed her legs and tapped him lightly with her heels. "You are okay. Nothing is going to hurt you."

A light breeze caused the horrid things to *bob* and *bump*. The cart got closer and closer. The rear wheel hung on a rock in the pavement and the cart stopped. The balloon man pushed harder. The cart jerked and clattered. It rolled towards Taz again.

Closer and closer.

Taz spun around in a circle, but there was no place for him to go. Stephanie pulled tight on the reins. Taz spun around in the other direction. People were everywhere. Tall buildings blocked his view.

Stephanie had not showed him big FLOATY things. He only knew about big FLAPPY things.

"Taz, whoa!" commanded Stephanie. Her voice was strong, but controlling. She pulled on his reins and backed him a few steps.

Taz decided to trust his rider. He sensed that his leader remained calm. He took one skittery step forward. And then another.

Finally, they were past that horrible balloon cart.

It wasn't that much farther until they made it to the end of the parade route.

Stephanie hopped to the ground and hugged his neck. She showered praises upon her beautiful, black Hackney. "You did so good, Taz. I am so proud of you," she said as she gave him a pat. "You are such a good boy."

Taz liked doing good. He liked making Stephanie happy. The Veteran's Day Parade was over and he had done his job.

He wanted to go home. He wanted to see Bly. He really missed his feed bucket, but he did not know how far away from home they were.

"We have to ride back to the trailer, Taz." Stephanie climbed on his back. "There's going to be people, cars, and floats, and you might see some scary things again."

Taz held his head high and waited for the signal from his rider to go ahead.

He could do this.

He had done it before.

As a matter of fact, he had ridden in his first parade only a few minutes ago. Getting back to the trailer was no big deal.

THE END

FUN FACTS ABOUT
Veteran's Day

- Veteran's Day came from "Armistice Day", November 11, 1919, which was the first anniversary of the end of World War I.
- A 1926 Congressional Resolution was passed for an annual observance.
- Veteran's Day became a national holiday in 1938.
- The purpose of Veteran's Day is to pay tribute and give thanks to all American veterans, especially those living today who have served or who are in active duty serving their country.

FUN FACTS ABOUT
The Pledge of Allegiance

- The original Pledge of Allegiance to the Flag was written in 1892 by Francis Bellamy.
- In 1923, the following words were added: "the flag of the United States of America."
- In 1942, the pledge was formally adopted by Congress.
- In 1949, Congress passed legislation to establish Flag Day as June 14.
- In 1954, President Eisenhower encouraged the addition of "under God", and the words were added through a joint resolution of Congress.

FUN FACTS ABOUT
The Colors of Our Flag

- In 1782 the colors red, white, and blue were adopted for the great seal as those *used in the flag of the United States of America.*
- Red for hardiness and valor.
- White for purity and innocence.
- Blue for vigilance, perseverance, and justice.
- The Secretary of State is the official custodian of the great seal, which is used on all official documents of the United States government.

FUN FACTS ABOUT
the Hackney Horse Breed

- The American Hackney Horse Society (AHHS) was formed in 1891, with headquarters today located in the Kentucky Horse Park in Lexington, Kentucky. The Society maintains a current registry of the Hackney breed.
- The origins of the Hackney breed are traced back to Norfolk, England, where the horses called Norfolk Trotters were bred for elegant style and speed. Combined with the Norfolk mares to sires of the Thoroughbred, the Hackney became a notable breed for carriage driving. Today's Hackney horses compete in Dressage, Trail Riding, Hunter/Jumper, and English Pleasure, in addition to other competitive events.
- The Hackney is on the list as being one of the ten rarest equine breeds.

CONTRIBUTORS

Natalie Bright, Author, Blogger, and Speaker, writes about the history, life, and people of Texas and the western frontier. Her articles have appeared in a variety of publications. She is the author of several book series for children and young adults. Sign up for a FREE eNewsletter on her website to receive excerpts of newest releases, and to find out about upcoming book events where you can meet Taz. http://nataliebright.com

Stephanie Nelson, owner/trainer, works as a dispatcher for a trucking company, and in her spare time volunteers at several animal rescue shelters. She has been riding ever since she can remember and loves working with rescue horses. TAZ is a registered Hackney from Panhandle Safe Hayven Equine Rescue. He was saved by the Sheriff's Department and brought to the shelter as a young horse, starved and very ill. Taz recovered nicely, loves his

adopted family, and continues to have an obsession with his food. It is true – he meets Stephanie at the fence line holding his feed bucket in his mouth.

Denise McAllister, Editor, has been writing stories since she was 10 years old. A business editor for the past 20+ years, she edits publications and websites for global corporations in Austria, Finland, and the U.S. Although she has worked on beautiful Hilton Head Island, SC as a communications coordinator/editor, Denise's heart is drawn to horses and anything Western. She writes  contemporary Western fiction and nonfiction, book reviews, and has edited books for members of the Western Writers of America organization.

Phillip Gessert, Graphic Design and Formatting, lent his talent to the book cover and layout design. http://www.gessertbooks.com

Panhandle Safe Hayven Horse Rescue, in Amarillo, Texas, is dedicated to educating the public about proper horse care, tirelessly working to save and improve the lives of equine in the Texas Panhandle and the surrounding area. To learn more about how you can help the people who care for and shelter these amazing animals, go here: http://panhandlehorserescue.com/

CONNECT WITH
us Online!

- **Follow Taz and Bly on Instagram:**
  https://www.instagram.com/tazandbly/

Find Natalie online here:

- Website: http://www.nataliebright.com
- Twitter: https://twitter.com/natNKB
- Instagram: https://www.instagram.com/natsgrams/
- Pinterest: https://www.pinterest.com/natbright/
- Facebook: https://www.facebook.com/
  nataliebrightauthor/
- LinkedIn: https://www.linkedin.com/in/natalie-
  bright-b451472b/

Please help other readers find this book by recommending it to your family, friends, educators, book clubs, and readers' groups. Let us know what you think. We would really appreciate your time in leaving an online review.

Need a program for your group or club relating to Natalie's books or about writing and publishing? Contact information and program synopsis can be found at http://nataliebright.com

CPSIA information can be obtained
at www.ICGtesting.com
Printed in the USA
LVHW02s1118210618
581173LV00016B/55/P

9 780998 810133